Suffolk Beaches

Steve & Alyson Appleyard

Published in 2011 by Red Flannel Publishing

Plumtree House, Mill Lane, East Runton

Norfolk NR27 9PH

www.redflannelpublishing.co.uk

Copyright © 2011 Steve & Alyson Appleyard

The right of Steve & Alyson Appleyard to be identified

as the authors of this work has been asserted by them

in accordance with the Copyright, Designs and

Patents Act 1988

ISBN 978-0-9561346-2-2

Printed by Barnwell Print Ltd, Aylsham, Norfolk

Introduction

The coastline of Suffolk is 47 miles long and within it we have deemed there to be 34 individual beaches. In some respects this is an arbitrary number, since of course many of the beaches run into each other, but we consider that each beach included here has a uniqueness about it, allowing it to be given the status of an individual beach. Our dictionary defines a beach to be - the shore of a sea or lake, especially when sandy or pebbly. With just a couple of exceptions all these beaches are composed of sand or shingle - but we have added a couple that are not - but these 'shores' are also well worth visiting.

What has been surprising is the amazing variation in the beaches, given that the Suffolk coast covers such a small part of the UK coastline. What is also surprising is the feeling of remoteness when you are on some of the beaches, considering that you are never far from a town or village.

We hope that you enjoy reading *Suffolk Beaches* and looking at the photographs - but we particularly recommend that you experience Suffolk beaches for yourself - all of them.

The 34 beaches and shores of Suffolk

1. Corton
2. Gunton
3. Lowestoft - North Denes
4. Lowestoft - North
5. Lowestoft - South
6. Pakefield
7. Kessingland
8. Benacre
9. Covehithe

10. Easton Bavents
11. Southwold - North
12. Southwold - South
13. Walberswick
14. Dunwich
15. Dunwich Heath
16. Minsmere
17. Sizewell
18. Thorpeness
19. Aldeburgh
20. Orford
21. Orford Ness
22. Havergate Island

23. Butley Ferry
24. Shingle Street
25. Bawdsey - North
26. Bawdsey - South
27. Bawdsey Quay
28. Old Felixstowe
29. Felixstowe
30. Landguard Point
31. Trimley Marshes
32. Nacton Shore
33. Orwell Country Park
34. Shotley Point

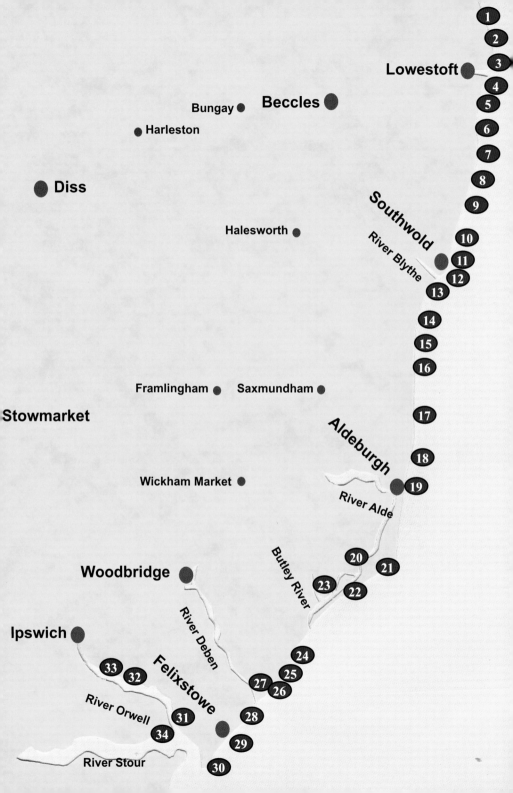

① Corton

Corton is the most northerly village on the Suffolk coast and the first of the thirty four beaches that make up the coastline. We do however get off to a rather inauspicious start, as access to the beach directly from Corton village has now been closed because of cliff erosion. Nor can you walk along the beach from Norfolk's most southerly beach at Hopton, because of the problems with erosion. We do not know if there are plans to rectify this situation in the future.

Fortunately for Corton it has another beach, just to the south of the village where there is an access slope - opposite the entrance to a golf course on the B1385 (where there is free parking). This beach was a designated naturists beach, but this designation has been withdrawn following the closure of the beach to the north. However it would appear that many naturists continue to use the beach - some very discretely as those behind the windbreak in the picture below - others less so.

1 Corton

As well as the official path down to the beach opposite the car park (known as Tramp's Alley), there are other sandy tracks that people use to get down to the beach from the road. Along the cliff top south from here there are very pleasant paths through the gorse and ferns, with clearings which make attractive and sheltered picnic spots. The wooded cliff top north of Tramp's Alley is a campsite with the entrance directly from the B1385 - with some very quiet pitches in the trees.

Corton 1

The golf course with the free parking is actually a pay and play pitch and putt course (9 hole Par 3) owned by Waveney District Council and known as Dip Farm. It is in an attractive position and appears to be very well maintained. From this car park there is access to the Corton Wood nature reserve also owned by Waveney District Council. It has a variety of mature trees including oak, ash, sycamore and beech and woodland flowers such as bluebells, lesser celandine and greater stitchwort.

② Gunton

The village of Gunton is now a northern suburb of Lowestoft and the beach is accessed down Links Road which is a turning off Corton Road - signed to North Beach. At the bottom of Links Drive there is a large free car park (bottom left) which is an excellent place from which to sit and watch the sea. The beach we are depicting here is to the north (left) of the car park. In the picture below, Gunton Cliffs can be seen in the distance - with Corton beyond that. Further south the cliffs become less steep and this area is known as Gunton Warren.

Gunton ②

Gunton Warren has been declared a Local Nature Reserve and it has a wide range of plant types, including cliff top scrub, heath, woodland and grassland. The area between the Warren and the beach is known as Gunton Denes - the word denes means "a sandy tract" - a similar if not the same meaning as the word dunes. It is a good area for dog walking, but this is often to the annoyance of the local birders, since it is also an excellent area for bird watching - with regular sightings of red-backed shrike.

③ Lowestoft - North Denes

Here we are looking at Lowestoft's coastline stretching north from the port area. A new defensive sea wall with promenade has been built which stretches some two kilometres northwards. The remains of the old sea defences can be seen on the seaward side of the promenade and these litter the beach making it very hazardous to venture on to the beach. The grassy area inland of the promenade and shown in the bottom photograph, is known as North Denes. For many years it was a caravan site but has been unused more recently - however it is reported that it will once again be developed as a caravan park.

Lowestoft - North Denes ③

At the north end of the promenade is a large car park (top picture) which can be accessed directly from Corton Road via Links Road. As the middle picture shows, the beach is much wider at this point but there are still lots of hazards in the sea. It is a good place to park and simply gaze out to sea, or to walk a dog in the area between the promenade and the cliffs. The southern end of the the promenade is accessed from Gas Works Road and passes behind factories on an industrial area (bottom picture). There is a limited amount of car parking here.

③ Lowestoft - North Denes

Lowestoft is the most easterly town in Britain and its most easterly part is known as Ness Point, where there is a unique circular platform called the Euroscope. This shows directions and distances to major European towns - and while you are standing on it, you are at that moment in time the most easterly person in Britain. The Euroscope is at the southern end of the promenade which is reached from Gas Works Road - there is a limited amount of parking nearby. Another landmark here is Suffolk's first wind turbine standing 80m high.

Lowestoft - North Denes ③

Other features in the North Denes area include Lowestoft's excellent maritime museum and a lighthouse which was one of the first to be established by Trinity House. The present tower dates from 1874. The maritime museum is in Sparrow's Nest Park which also has a a children's play area, a cafe and Britain's most easterly bar. Sparrow's Nest Park is in Whapload Road which has both roadside parking and a car park at its northend - which gives direct access to the North Denes.

④ Lowestoft - North

Lowestoft is justifiably proud of its two award winning beaches. North Beach stretches from Claremont Pier northwards to South Pier - which is the entrance to the harbour. Both of the Lowestoft beaches south of the harbour hold prestigious Blue Flag awards and they are in fact the only beaches in Suffolk to have achieved this very high standard. Lowestoft is very much a seaside holiday destination and the beaches are a focal point of this. Given the right weather you can be sure of a most enjoyable beach holiday here.

Lowestoft - North

4 Lowestoft - North

A wide promenade runs the full length of North Beach with seats on which to sit and gaze out to sea and to watch the activity on the beach. There is a lifeguard lookout and in the season there is a high visibility of lifeguards - on one of the mornings I visited there was clearly a training exercise being conducted, which showed me just how proficient they are. At the southern end of this beach is Claremont Pier which contains an amusement arcade, but the open pier beyond is inaccessible and appears to be unsafe. You can walk along South Pier which is at the north end of the beach - this forms one side of the harbour entrance. There is much to see at this northern end of the beach which is closest to the town centre.

The visible part of the harbour is now a yacht marina and within this is the Mincarlo, a fishing trawler that is open to the public and well worth a visit. In the area at the north end of the beach, known as Royal Plain, is the East Point Pavilion Visitor Centre and a fun fountain area where 74 jets of water shoot up randomly, to the amusement of children who can run amongst them. There is an events area in the gardens adjacent to the promenade and during one of our visits there was a children's entertainer keeping everyone amused. There is plenty of car parking adjacent to the gardens and beach.

⑤ Lowestoft - South

Lowestoft's South Beach (which is south of Claremont Pier) has the prestigious Blue Flag award and as can be seen from the photographs below and opposite, taken early in the morning, it a most impressive looking beach. Clearly the beach is raked and cleaned in the summer, so that it looks fresh and inviting each morning. Behind the beach is a promenade along which there are colourful traditional beach huts that can be hired on a daily, weekly or seasonal basis. Along the promenade is the beach office and also the lifeguard station from which the lifeguards operate in the peak season. At the southern end of the beach, as you get closer to Pakefield, there are small areas where Marram grass is growing.

⑥ Pakefield

If you walk from the well groomed South Beach of Lowestoft to Pakefield, you will find the most dramatic of contrasts. Pakefield with its boats, fishermen's huts and the old machinery used to pull the boats up the beach, it is as if time has passed it by. I personally found it very appealing and charming. Although most of the original fishing village has long been swallowed up by the sea, Pakefield still has a character of its own.

Pakefield

The skyline at Pakefield is dominated by the church which has stood here for more than one thousand years. The Parish Church of All Saints' and St Margaret's is unusual because it was originally built as two "semi-detached" churches, hence the double name. At some point in its history it was opened up into one church, with two almost identical knaves and chancels. The church has a thatched roof which was badly damaged by incendiary bombs in the war but now restored.

⑥ Pakefield

There is a path running along the cliff top with benches at regular intervals to sit and admire the seaward view - or you can do this from the comfort and shelter of your car in the cliff top car park. One website about Pakefield refers to its six pubs - we neither counted or tried them, although the two closest to the beach looked rather welcoming - as did the fish and chip shop! The same website referred to the long line shore sea angling and we certainly saw exponents of this.

⑦ Kessingland

There used to be two separate communities known as the "Street" and the "Beach", but new building in the sixties has effectively combined them into one village. The sea is virtually out of sight, even when you are at the most easterly point of the village, because of a wide expanse of grassland and shingle which you have to cross to reach the shingle beach. There is very little car parking from which to directly access this area. The only public car park being almost one mile back towards the village centre. At the closest point to the beach there are public toilets and an attractive looking restaurant called The Waterfront. Much of the frontage here is taken up by a caravan park. Kessingland beach has a Quality Coast Award from the Keep Britain Tidy Organisation.

Kessingland

7 Kessingland

Kessingland

A promenade runs northwards from the beach access road for almost half a mile. This forms part of the Suffolk Coastal Path. The southern extremity of Kessingland beach is bounded by Benacre pumping station at the outfall of the Hundred River - almost one mile from the beach access point

⑧ Benacre

As you head south from Kessingland and cross the Hundred River near the pumping station, you enter Benacre National Nature Reserve. The sign at this point advises - "This National Nature Reserve was established by Natural England with the Benacre Estate, to foster the diverse and rare wildlife of this internationally important site. The wildlife is dependent on the extensive range of habitats which includes reedbed, woods, grasslands, heath and beach as well as both fresh and salt water. The coastal lagoons are some of the finest in Europe".

The lake seen in the top photograph opposite (with the pumping station in the background) was one of three gravel pits created in the last war, for the construction of runways and pill boxes. The other two have been lost to the sea through erosion. This one is home to little grebes and little egrets as well as migratory birds.

⑧ Benacre

As you head further south you ultimately arrive at a lake known as Benacre Broad as seen in the middle and bottom photographs opposite. This is approximately one mile south of the pumping station. Just prior to this is the unusual site of trees, which were once growing on the now eroded cliffs, continuing to defy the sea. You have to be careful on this last stretch, as the sea comes right up to the cliffs at high tide and so it is important to be aware of the tide times. The Suffolk Coastal Path actually heads inland at the gravel pits and passes inland of Benacre Broad. If the tide is right you can continue southwards for a further mile to Covehithe. There is no direct car access to the beach here - the village of Benacre is approximately one mile to the west. If you can find somewhere to park then you could walk back along the coastal path.

⑨ Covehithe

The village of Covehithe or rather what remains of it, truly is the end of the line as the road from Wrentham simply disappears over the fast eroding cliffs. Fortunately there is a ample warning of this - the sign advises that there is neither a right of way or pedestrian access to the beach. Covehithe is now comprised of just a couple of houses and the thatched church of St Andrew, which was built in 1672 within the ruins of a larger church - suggesting just how large the village was at one time. While there is no access to the beach along the original road, there is a marked footpath on the south side of the road just inland from the church. There is a limited amount of parking close to the start of the footpath. The half mile walk to the beach crosses more of the Benacre National Nature Reserve and you finally emerge on to a fine sandy beach at the point where the cliffs disappear.

⑨ Covehithe

The beach is wide at the point where the path arrives and also here is Covehithe Broad, which is fenced off to protect the ground nesting birds. As you walk both northwards to Benacre, or southwards to Southwold, the beach narrows and the cliffs rise. At high tide the sea reaches up to the cliffs so care should be taken to observe the tide times. Southwold can be seen in the distance in the middle photo opposite and Covehithe church can just be seen in the bottom picture.

⑩ Easton Bavents

This section of beach stretches northwards from Southwold for two miles to Easton Woods. At this point the cliifs have given way to Easton Broad, which is part of a nature reserve and is home to a number of breeding shore birds. The cliffs rise again to the south of Easton Broad and are probably the fastest eroding in Suffolk. A number of houses have been lost in recent years and the owners of those under threat have been pursuing various high profile legal actions. There is no direct access to this beach other than to walk from Southwold or Covehithe, but care should be taken as the sea comes right up to the cliffs at high tide.

⑪ Southwold - North

Southwold is a delightful and unspoilt seaside town with more than one and a half miles of excellent beach. We have arbitrarily split the beach into north and south of the pier, but this means that the majority of the beach comes under Southwold South - with only a few hundred yards of beach lying north of the pier. However in this section we have included the pier itself and also the boating lake and model boat pool, which are adjacent to the northern section of the beach - as too is Southwold's main car park. These are all behind the beach huts shown in these photographs. We have taken the northern limit of Southwold beach to be the last of the stone groynes - after this is the beach of Easton Bavents, which can be seen in the distance in the photograph below. The image also shows the sweep of Sole Bay. In the 17th Century Southwold was the main anchorage for the English fleet, with the town a great attraction for the sailors. In 1672 the Dutch fleet attacked the English fleet at anchor and the battle of Sole Bay ensued. Hundreds of bodies were subsequently washed up and many of the dead and wounded were landed at Southwold.

⑪ Southwold - North

Southwold can be proud of its pier, which has been fully restored in recent years with the addition of shops and cafe's - all in keeping with the charm of Southwold. There is also an amusement arcade on the pier called "The under the pier show" featuring whacky exhibits designed by Tim Hunkin - the clock below was also designed by him. As mentioned, in the area north of the pier is a large model boat pond and a children's boating pond which is overlooked by a tearoom which serves excellent scones.

⑫ Southwold - South

Southwold beach south of the pier stretches for 2km to the mouth of the River Blyth. It is in effect two beaches - the first one kilometre is directly adjacent to the town centre and is backed by a promenade and beach huts. Within the area of the first three groynes immediately south of the pier, the beach has been awarded the Quality Coast Award. The second kilometre of the beach, which extends south from the end of the promenade, is known as Southwold Denes beach. The photographs on these two pages show this most popular first one kilometre, with the town rising behind and Southwold's iconic lighthouse. It is a popular beach with generally safe bathing - particularly within the award area - provided you keep away from the groynes and do not swim when there are warning flags.

⑫ Southwold - South

The photographs below show the Denes section of the beach, which widens as it extends from the end of the promenade and beach huts. This part of the beach has a Quality Coast Award for its entire length - although its designation is as a non-bathing beach, as there is no lifeguard cover. The beach is backed by sand dunes which can offer shelter on windy days and behind them is the road to the harbour. The beach ends at the entrance to the River Blythe, upstream is the harbour area with moorings for both pleasure and commercial fishing boats. There are numerous wooden buildings from which the catch is sold, as well as fish retaurants - this is an area not to be missed when you visit Southwold. A rowing boat ferry provides a regular service across the river to the village of Walberswick.

⑬ Walberswick

The beach at Walberswick starts on the southern side of the River Blyth - the top photograph below is looking north towards the pier structure that forms the entrance to the river - as shown in the top photograph opposite. The bottom photograph on this page is the view south, showing the curve of the coast towards Dunwich. The beach, which is backed by sand dunes, is a few hundred metres from the village and Walberswick's car park. Walberswick is a beautiful and popular village and even though the car park is large it can become full in the summer.

⑬ Walberswick

Many day visitors to Walberswick do not choose to visit the beach, but instead spend their time near the river and creek - crabbing. As can be seen in the photographs opposite, everyone - young and old alike - gets the crabbing bug when they visit Walberswick. For the past thirty years Walberswick has held the British Open Crabbing Championship in August. As can be seen in the bottom photograph (courtesy of the Crabbing Championship) it is a hugely popular event - raising lots of money for charities. The winner is the person catching the largest crab. There is a rowing boat ferry that crosses the river to Southwold, as well as a footbridge approximately one kilometre upstream. As already mentioned, Walberswick is a charming village with tea rooms, restaurants, two pubs, an art gallery and craft and gift shops.

⑭ Dunwich

We understand that Dunwich was one of the largest ports in Eastern England and the tenth largest place in the country, with a population of around 3000. It was also a religious centre, having some eight churches. In 1286 a large storm swept much of the town into the sea and a further storm in 1328 destroyed the harbour. Subsequent storms caused further losses so that there is little left of Dunwich standing today - however it is still well worth visiting. Of the original buildings there are only the ruins of the 13th century Fransciscan friary on the edge of the cliff and Leper Hospital chapel in the present churchyard. Of the newer buildings, the two most prominent are the excellent 17th century Ship Inn and the Dunwich Museum, where you can learn more about the Dunwich story.

Dunwich 14

The beach is for the most part shingle, forming a shingle bank which stretches northwards to Walberswick. To the south there are cliffs which are soft and still eroding. Behind the beach is a large car park within which is the famous Flora Tearooms (the large wooden building in the photograph below). People travel huge distances for their superb fish and chips.

⑮ Dunwich Heath

The beach here is accessed by taking a path down from Dunwich Heath - which covers a large area spreading inland from the cliff top. The beach is shingle and to the north is backed by the cliffs which arose from the car park at Dunwich. To the south the cliffs quickly disappear. Dunwich Heath is a particularly beautiful stretch of the Suffolk coast within an 'Area of Outstanding Natural Beauty' owned by the National Trust. The heath is covered by magnificent pink and purple flowering heather from late June until September and a further splash of colour is provided by the yellow gorse. Way marked trails criss-cross the heath as does the Suffolk Coast Path. Quoting from the National Trust information, there are - guided walks, family nature trails, Tracker Packs, smugglers' and history trails, tea-room events, sea watching and wildlife identification charts and telescopes. The literature goes on to say that Dunwich Heath offers you peace and quiet and a true sense of being at one with nature - and we would certainly not disagree with this. The tea room, a gift shop and the lookout are all housed within old coastguard buildings.

Dunwich Heath

⑮ Dunwich Heath

16 Minsmere

This beach forms part of the RSPB's Minsmere reserve and an area is cordoned off to protect nesting little terns. A visit to the reserve is highly recommended, particularly in spring when you can watch avocets and marsh harriers and perhaps hear booming bitterns. There are nature trails and hides and an excellent visitor centre with shop and tearoom. It is a very family friendly place with special activity days for children, as well as the year round availability of family explorer backpacks and trail booklets.

⑰ Sizewell

Without the need to visit every beach in Suffolk for the purpose of writing this book, I would probably have never visited Sizewell - deterred of course by the presence of two nuclear power stations. I would now simply say - don't be put off. The power stations are of course a presence, both on land and in the sea - the latter in the form of two structures which are presumably where the cooling water is collected and discharged. However you simply get used to their presence and for me they did not unduly detract from my enjoyment of the beach. The sea structures are an added bonus if sea angling is your thing - we understand from fishing websites that they are like a magnet to fish drawing in many varieties, including bass and sole. The nearest of the structures known as Outlet A is apparently reachable with a good cast from the beach. As can be seen from the photographs, Sizewell beach is mostly shingle with sand dunes and grass behind. There is a path directly across the dunes to the beach and others run parallel providing lots of opportunity for walking. The fishing boats on the beach and the old fishermen's huts provide colour and character to the the area.

⑰ Sizewell

There is a memorial comprising a pair of bronze oars overlooking the beach, with the following inscription on one of the blades -

"In memory of the thirty-two young Dutchmen who tried to escape to England by kayak during World War II to join the allied forces. Eight of them reached the English coast. Only three survived the war. The last living survivor dedicated this memorial to his brothers in arms who were less fortunate. He reached England - and freedom - on this beach on 21 September 1941".

There is a carpark on the edge of the sand dunes, with an elevated position from where you can enjoy the sea views. The Sizewell Beach Refreshment Cafe is also on the edge of the dunes and there is a local pub - the Vulcan Arms.

⑱ Thorpeness

The beach at Thorpeness is wide and for the most part shingle. Although it is popular in the summer, it is not its beach for which this holiday village is famed. Thorpeness was created in the 1920's as a private fantasy holiday village by Glencairn Stuart Ogilvie a wealthy Scottish barrister and entrepreneur. The village features a golf course, a windmill, a boating lake, and numerous holiday homes which were built in Jacobean and Tudor styles. Another feature is the "House in the Clouds" - which was built to disguise the eyesore of the village water tower. The tank was clad in wood to make it look like a house on the top of a five storey tower, which itself is a house - now available for holiday rent.

The favourite place for most visitors to Thorpeness is the boating lake - known as the Meare. The Meare covers an area of some sixty acres including many islands, which have been named after characters and locations - and incorporate features from - Peter Pan. There over 100 boats for hire including rowing boats, canoes and sailing boats. Boating on the Meare is both popular and safe, as nowhere is it more than one metre deep.

Thorpeness 18

18 Thorpeness

⑲ Aldeburgh

Aldeburgh is a totally unspoilt seaside town with lots of character and renowned for its annual festival of music and other arts. The beach is a wide shingle bank with houses and hotels facing directly on to it. Fishing boats on the beach and fishermen's huts add character - as well as providing the opportunity to purchase freshly caught local fish and of course excellent fish and chips. As with other places along this stretch of coast, much of Aldeburgh has been lost to the sea, having once had a flourishing ship building industry. However unlike Dunwich there is still much of Aldeburgh left, including the Moot Hall which was built in 1650 and a windmill which faces the beach on the southern edge of the town - now converted in to a home. On the beach at the northern edge of the town is *The Scallop* a sculpture dedicated to Benjamin Britten, who used to walk along the beach in the afternoons. The stainless steel sculpture stands four metres high and was created by Maggi Hambling a local Suffolk based artist. It carries the words *"I hear those voices that will not be drowned"*.

⑲ Aldeburgh

Aldeburgh stands on the River Alde which is to the south of the town, but it does not actually enter the sea until a point some ten miles further south - at the southern end of Orfordness. A track heads south from Aldeburgh - with the sea on your left and the river on your right, passing Slaughden Quay where there are a couple of yacht clubs and from where a boat takes passengers on trips to explore the upper reaches of the Alde. Slaughden was another of those fishing villages now completely lost to the sea. Continuing further south on this track you will see a Martello Tower, it is the most northerly of these defensive towers - built to resist a possible Napoleonic invasion. If you continued further south you would enter Orfordness, but you are prohibited from doing so.

⓴ Orford

Orford just about qualifies to be in this book by virtue of its tiny beach shown in the photograph below, but it has to be in any book about the Suffolk coast since it is from here that both Orfordness and Havergate Island are accessed. Orford stands on the River Ore which is the River Alde as it flows down from Snape via Aldeburgh, but changes its name as it passes Orford and then flows on to reach the sea at Shingle Street. From Orford the National Trust operate a regular ferry across to Orford Ness and the RSPB operates a boat to take visitors to its reserve at Havergate Island. A local operator runs one hour trips around Havergate island on his boat the *Regardless*. The larger vessel shown in the photograph overleaf is the ex fishing boat the *Lady Florence* which also sails from Orford and offers the opportunity to dine while you cruise the river.

Orford is an historic village . The village website informs us that in the Middle Ages it was a thriving sea port from where Eleanor of Aquitaine set off to ransom her son Richard the Lion Heart. The 12th century Orford Castle was built by Henry II and is now owned by English Heritage and is open to the public.

㉑ Orford Ness

Orford Ness is a ten mile long shingle spit with an area of marsh, lagoons and creeks and owned by the National Trust. It is at its narrowest where it joins the coast just south of Aldeburgh and where it is virtually only the width of the track which runs on to it - as shown in the top picture opposite. However there is no access to the public at this point. The only public access on to Orfordness Ness is from the quay at Orford, from where the National trust operates a ferry across the River Ore. The middle picture opposite is taken from the top of Orford Castle - from where you can see the lighthouse and other features of this very strange place. Orfordness was a secret military testing site through the two world wars and in the period after WWII, when key elements of Britain's nuclear weapons were tested here. For information, the beach is shingle as shown below, but it is not a place for swimming as there are dangerous currents just offshore. The tower is a lookout post used by the security police until the perimeter fence was removed in 1993. When you visit Orfordness there are three marked trails, which take in both the wildlife areas as well as passing the many derelict buildings.

㉑ Orford Ness

Orford Ness is a quiet and almost eyrie place with many derelict buildings and rusting artefacts abandoned by those who worked here. On the top of one of the buildings is a pair of high powered binoculars, from where you can see across the flat terrain for many miles. The building in the middle picture opposite is known as the Black Beacon and was used for testing experimental aircraft navigation beacons. The bottom picture is one of six laboratories used for the testing of components for nuclear bombs. One of the old accommodation buildings is used as an exhibition area, with display boards explaining what went on at Orfordness in the past.

㉒ Havergate Island

Havergate which is in the Ore estuary, is the only island on the Suffolk coast. It is two miles long and approximately half a mile wide at its widest point. It is an important nature reserve with habitats including saline lagoons, saltmarsh, mudflats, shingle and grazing marsh. Havergate Island is owned and managed by the RSPB and the only way of reaching it is on their boat - which only takes visitors across on the first Saturday of each month and booking via the centre at the RSPB Minsmere reserve is essential. However you can view the island by taking a one hour boat trip on the *"Regardless"* - which sails from the quay at Orford on a regular basis. Havergate is famous for its breeding avocets and terns, which can usually be seen in the spring and summer. In autumn and winter, the island is home to a large number of ducks and wading birds. There is also a population of brown hare. Havergate Island and the River Ore can be clearly seen from the top of Orford Castle as shown in the picture below.

㉓ Butley Ferry

The Suffolk Coast Path extends for some fifty miles from Felixstowe to Lowestoft. At a number of points the path has to come inland to circumvent rivers and here we have focussed on the path as it passes inland on the south side of the Butley River - which itself is a tributary of the River Ore. The path continues inland to also pass round the River Alde before returning to continue up the coast at Aldeburgh. As you head inland on the south side of the Butley River opposite the southern end of Havergate Island, you pass through the RSPB's Boyton Marsh nature reserve and you also pass the wooden jetties of Butley ferry. A ferry has operated here since the 16th century and a ferry service has started once again - manned by volunteers and supported by the Alde & Ore Association. A nearby sign advises that the ferry was started in the late 16th century by local landowner Robert Forth. Successive landowners continued to operate the ferry including two widows, one a mother of ten children - it finally stopped in 1932. Presently the volunteers operate it from 11.00 to 16.00 on Saturdays, Sundays and Bank Holidays from Easter Saturday until the end of September.

23 Butley Ferry

Butley Ferry 23

24 Shingle Street

Few places can be better described by their name - Shingle Street is one road with a single row of houses, which face out directly on to the wide shingle beach and the sea. Shingle Street is located at the centre of Hollesley Bay, at the mouth of the River Ore (which becomes the River Alde after Orford and has the Butley River as a tributary). The entrance to the river can be seen in the distance in the picture below. There appear to be potentially dangerous shingle banks approaching the entrance and presumably great care has to be taken by vessels entering the river to keep to the buoyed channel. There are no shops or tea rooms at Shingle Street, just a few houses and some of these are holiday homes and so for much of the time it appears to be virtually deserted. There are numerous stories and theories of incidents that may have happened here in the last war, including evidence that indicates that there may have been a foiled German invasion attempt in 1940.

24 Shingle Street

Shingle Street
Site of Special Scientific Interest

The land and track beyond this sign are privately owned by
the bungalow known as "The Beacons"

Shingle Street is Special

Only you can keep it that way

DO NOT DRIVE BEYOND THIS POINT

PLEASE RESPECT WILDLIFE AND THE PRIVACY
OF THE RESIDENTS OF "THE BEACONS"

* Suffolk County Council
01473 583000

* The Landowners

WARNING
Strong Currents

Unsuitable
for
Bathing

㉕ Bawdsey - North

This beach at Bawdsey is approximately one kilometre down East Lane, which is a turning at the southern end of the village. There is a limited amount of parking near to some WWII defensive structures. There is no direct access to the beach here or to the south, because of erosion and newly constructed sea defences which should not be climbed on. East Lane is actually part of the Suffolk Coast Path which has detoured inland but then follows the coast northwards. After a few hundred metres travelling north you can access the beach. This is a huge shingle bank which you can see in the picture below, stretching northwards to Shingle Street and the River Ore.

㉖ Bawdsey - South

This section of Bawdsey beach is just north of the River Deben and you can walk to it from Bawdsey quay. It was of particular interest to me, as you get a good view of Bawdsey Manor from here and one of my interests is radar and its early wartime developments. The concept of radar was demonstrated at Orfordness in 1935 and a development team was then moved to Bawdsey Manor, lead by Robert Watson-Watt. 360ft high towers were erected and Bawdsey became the first Chain Home Radar Station. By the outbreak of the war a chain of radar stations was in place around the coast of Britain. Today Bawdsey Manor is used for courses, conferences and weddings. A group of enthusiasts is currently restoring the original Transmitter Block which is open to the public on certain Sundays in the year.

27 Bawdsey Quay

Bawdsey Quay is a further two miles after passing through the village of Bawdsey and is literally the end of the road. There is a small car park and also some parking along the road, from where there are excellent views of the River Deben. Along this stretch of the north side of the Deben there are small areas of beach, initially sandy and then becoming shingle towards the mouth of the estuary. There is a foot ferry across the river to Old Felixstowe, which you summon by waving a round white board. The Boathouse Cafe is worthy of a visit.

㉘ Old Felixstowe

This beach is at the most northerly point of Felixstowe, accessed by car along Cliff Road or by walking along what is the Stour and Orwell Walk. There is a conveniently located cliff top car park in an area known as Clifflands, from where you can sit in your car and look seaward or take the steps down to the shingle beach. From here you can continue to walk northwards for approximately one mile - or you can drive across the golf course - until you reach the River Deben and the hamlet of Felixstowe Ferry. Here there is another car park, boat yards, a pub (the Felixstowe Ferry), the Ferry Cafe and the foot ferry which takes you across the Deben to Bawdsey Quay.

㉙ Felixstowe

If you have never visited Felixstowe you may only imagine it as a large container port, rather than the impressive seaside resort that it is (the container port is tucked round the corner on the River Orwell). The beach at Felixstowe curves around a bay and is backed by a wide two mile long promenade. We have depicted the beach with photographs over the following six pages. The images on these two pages show the beach and promenade at its northerly end. Behind this section of the promenade are the attractive Cliff Gardens, which give Felixstowe the title of "The Garden Resort of East Anglia".

㉙ Felixstowe

The photographs on these two pages show the beach and promenade in the middle section of its two mile length - either side of the pier. Alongside this section there are children's rides, a boating lake and a swimming pool. Felixstowe pier which was once the longest in East Anglia is closed - presumably because it is unsafe - other than the amusement arcade at the shore end.

㉙ Felixstowe

These photographs show the beach and promenade along the southerly section of its two mile length. The beach is at its widest and is more sandy along this section and there are stone groynes which can offer shelter on the cooler windy days. There is more availability of car parking at this southern end of the beach.

Felixstowe

㉚ Landguard Point

Landguard Point is a shingle spit projecting out into the North Sea and with the River Orwell on its western side. From here there are excellent views of the shipping as it approaches the Felixstowe container port and the Harwich ferry port - if that is your interest. Much of the Point is a nature reserve of national importance, managed by the Suffolk Wildlife Trust. As one of their information boards states - over 450 species of plants have been recorded here, including a third of all British grasses. Landguard has also been of military significance dating back to the time of Henry VIII and there are remains of defence structures from past conflicts.

30 Landguard Point

Landguard Fort is a spectacular coastal artillery fort built in the 18th century with additions in both the 19th and 20th centuries - and in use until 1956. It is owned by English Heritage and is open to the public.

③① Trimley Marshes

I was interested to find out what the shores are like next to the Felixstowe container terminal on the River Orwell - shown on the O.S. map as Fagbury Point. Fortunately the Stour and Orwell Walk passes immediately behind the container terminal and then follows the river upstream on top of the river bank. Enroute you pass the Fagbury viewpoint, which gives views across the marshes. Then as you arrive at the river, you have the views of the shore shown in these two photographs - and those on the following pages. The view across the river is of Shotley Point and the Shotley marshes. The land in this area forms the Trimley Marshes nature reserve, owned and managed by the Suffolk Wildlife Trust and you should take time to visit the reserve and see the excellent work being carried out by the SWT. As the trust website says - "The mosaic of habitats, managed primarily for birds, makes this reserve one of the best sites in the county... The lagoon and its islands provide a variety of habitats throughout the year. The islands are ideal nesting sites for avocet, ringed plover and tufted duck".

Trimley Marshes

㉛ Trimley Marshes

32 Nacton Shore

There is part of the northern bank of the River Orwell which is shown on the O.S map as Nacton Shore and where there is a small car park and access for walking. At low tide there is a beach which stretches eastwards for a mile or so towards the sea and along which you can walk - returning on the Stour and Orwell Walk which passes through the edge of Home Wood.

Nacton Shore

③③ Orwell Country Park

"A rural oasis close to the heart of Ipswich" - was Cathy Brown's description of the Orwell Country Park in an article in the Suffolk Magazine. These photographs hopefully show that its beach contributes to the idyll - particularly on a perfect summer's day. Orwell Country Park covers more than 80 hectares on the north side of the River Orwell, literally in the shadow of the A14 road bridge. The park extends on both sides of the A14 road, but these photographs show just the seaward side. Some of the park falls within the Suffolk Coasts and Heaths Area of Outstanding Natural Beauty and it also includes Sites of Special Scientific Interest. Bridge Wood is incorporated within the park and is designated as an ancient woodland with a number of magnificent old English Oak trees that are more than 400 years old. The Stour and Orwell Walk which detoured inland at Nacton Shore returns to the river here - before heading in to Ipswich. At low tide you can walk along the beach returning through the wood - with stunning views of the river, framed by the trees.

33 Orwell Country Park

㉞ Shotley Point

This is the last beach in Suffolk - or the first of course if you are travelling north - and it is in the most unusual and dramatic position at Shotley Point, which is at the confluence of the rivers Orwell and Stour. From Shotley Point you look eastwards into the open water of Harwich Harbour, with Felixstowe to your left and Harwich to your right. The beach shown below is the south bank of the River Orwell, from where you look directly across to the Felixstowe container terminal and Trimley Marshes. The beach itself is part of Shotley Marshes and the path behind it is the the Stour and Orwell Walk, which follows the river all the way to Ipswich.

Shotley Point

A foot ferry operates from Shotley Point to Harwich and also from Harwich to Felixstowe and so you can reach this beach by ferry from either place - rather than the long drive around the Orwell or Stour. Curiously part of this beach was covered with shells - more than we have seen on any other beach in Suffolk.

34 Shotley Point

On a pleasant day you can sit at one of the tables of the Shipwreck pub and watch the shipping, or on a cold and windy day you can sit in your car in the nearby carpark which directly overlooks the water.

Shotley Point 34

This beach and picnic spot is just "round the corner" from Shotley Point on the northern bank of the River Stour, near to the village of Shotley Gate. The top photograph shows the view up the River Stour and the bottom photograph shows the view back to Harwich with Shotley Pier in the mid distance. There is a footpath along the north bank of the Stour which after three miles joins up with the Stour and Orwell Walk, which for some reason goes inland from Shotley Gate.

 # For further information

Suffolk County Council -
www.suffolk.gov.uk

Waveney District Council -
www.waveney.gov.uk

Suffolk Coastal District Council -
www.suffolkcoastal.gov.uk

Ipswich Borough Council -
www.ipswich.gov.uk

Suffolk Tourist Information Centres
Aldeburgh 01728 453637
atic@suffolkcoastal.gov.uk
Felixstowe 01394 276770
ftic@suffolkcoastal.gov.uk
Southwold 01502 724729
southwold.tic@waveney.gov.uk
Lowestoft 01502 533600
touristinfo@waveney.gov.uk
Woodbridge 01394 382240
wtic@suffolkcoast.gov.uk
Bury St Edmunds 01284 764667
tic@stedmundsbury.gov.uk
Ipswich 01473 258070
tourist@ipswich.gov.uk
Lavenham 01787 248207
lavenhamtic@babergh.gov.uk
Newmarket 01638 667200
tic.newmarket@forest-heath.gov.uk
Stowmarket 01449 676800
tic@midsuffolk.gov.uk
Sudbury 01787 881320
sudburytic@babergh.gov.uk

For further information

Lowestoft -
www.visit-sunrisecoast.co.uk
Felixstowe -
www.felixstowe.gov.uk

The National Trust -
www.nationaltrust.org.uk
Orford Ness - 01728 648024
Dunwich Heath - 01728 648501

RSPB -
www.rspb.org.uk
RSPB Minsmere Reserve - 01728 648281

Suffolk Wildlife Trust - 01473 890089
www.suffolkwildlifetrust.org

The Alde & Ore Association -
www.aldeandore.org

Thorpeness -
www.themeareatthorpeness.com
www.houseintheclouds.co.uk

www.suffolkcoastandheaths.org

www.bawdseyradar.org

www.boathousecafe.co.uk

www.southwoldpier.co.uk

www.aldeburgh-uk.com

www.pakefieldchurch.com

Battle of Solebay -
www.ship-wrecks.co.uk/battleofsolebay

www.dunwichmuseum.org.uk

Information on award beaches -
www.keepbritaintidy.org

British Open Crabbing Championship -
www.explorewalberswick.co.uk/crabbing

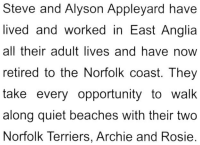

Steve and Alyson Appleyard have lived and worked in East Anglia all their adult lives and have now retired to the Norfolk coast. They take every opportunity to walk along quiet beaches with their two Norfolk Terriers, Archie and Rosie.